THE ART AND EFFICACY OF MANAGING
PERSON PERCEPTIONS

THE ART AND EFFICACY OF MANAGING PERSON PERCEPTIONS

Manipulation In The Highest Psychotherapeutic Sense

K.L. Fischer PhD

K.L. Fischer Publications

Publisher: K.L. Fischer Publications

ISBN-13: 978-1539338475

ISBN-10: 1539338479

What makes a person tick? We could be talking "time bomb" here. We could be talking physiologically here about someone's heart stressed beyond its capacity. Or we could be talking psychologically here about someone so angry they're about to explode. All emotions have a physiological component. Some illnesses are called psychosomatic because there are physiological effects brought on by psychological causes.

The psychiatrist would be particularly adept (at least one would think so) in treating such illnesses (I prefer to use the term disorders) since both psyche and soma (body) are involved. I can't even count the number of times I've been asked the question – What's the difference between a psychiatrist and a psychologist? I try to keep my response layman-like and in so doing probably short-change both sides. I tell them a psychiatrist is first of all an MD, who after obtaining their MD go on to do a three to four year residency studying the psyche in particular. A psychologist studies the psyche from day-one in their education and training – Four years undergrad; one and one half years for their Masters; another three to four years doing research; and a dissertation to receive their doctorate – PhD; and then 3,000 supervised hours to get their license to practice.

Psychiatrists who read my book may not like what I'm about to say (They're welcome to let me know about it). Psychiatrists are more well-equipped to treat disorders where something organic is being affected which in turn is impairing the psyche. As an MD they're in a better position to treat the organic, physiological components of the disorder than is the PhD psychologist. And of course, along with this particular expertise comes their biggest perk of all – Medication Management.

Psychologists do Psychotherapy i.e. Therapy for the Psyche – Hour-long psychotherapy sessions rather than 10 minute medication checks. The point of all of this is not, first and foremost, to antagonize psychiatrists (besides a small percentage of them do do psychotherapy), but rather help you, the lay person, make the wise choice where (and to whom) to turn for help. To be fair here, know that in some instances psychologists and psychiatrists work in concert treating the client – with the psychiatrist assessing the need for medication and, if it is needed, following up with the medication management. The psychologist, however, does the psychotherapy – How this ultimately plays out, when both professionals make the client's wellbeing their highest priority is that each professional respects the boundaries and limitations of each other's area of expertise.

Amongst psychologists there are diverse psychotherapeutic approaches to treating the client based upon the theoretical orientation of the therapist. It would be prudent for clients (right from the start) to ask the therapist what their orientation and approach to doing psychotherapy are. I've been doing psychotherapy as a practicing psychologist for the past thirty-five years and I must tell you, I typically don't wait for my client to ask me. I tell them right up-front in a plain, simple, straightforward way – What kind of therapist I am – What my orientation and approach are – So they have a pretty good idea what to expect and also have some idea (at least) whether it fits with what they need.

I tell them I'm a **Reality Therapist** – What's a reality therapist? Dare I state the obvious? A reality therapist is one who makes perceiving and presenting reality their highest priority. And just what is Reality? Reality is what the person-perceiving-what-is-reality-to-them says it is. What they're perceiving as real is real to them. Is this kind of reality subjective, idiosyncratic, one of a kind? You bet it is! **Objective Reality**, on the other hand is reality by consensus – perceivers of reality perceiving not quite the same thing, in not quite the same way, consenting to pool their perception to achieve something called objective reality.

A reality therapist concentrates on the NOW. The present. What's happening in the client's life is the subject matter in the session. The client's report is what the therapist relies upon – That, plus the therapist's own clinical perceptions. The client, of course, has their own perceptions of the other in their life and perceptions of how the other perceives them and perceptions of themselves. These are the perceptions that are real to the client. Clients tell their story based upon how they see it. The therapist tries to see the client's life the way the client sees it to get a feeling for what the client is feeling, so they can empathize with the client. I then give my clients insights. This fits with my cognitive-behavioral approach in which I use my perceptions of the client's situation to get their cognitive process going. I get them to think about their situation in a different way. Perhaps perceive things in a new way. Perhaps consider making some behavioral changes. The perhapses underscore the tentativeness of the process of changing. The client (though they might wish they could) can't take the therapist home with them. They are left to operate under their own power in dealing with the realities of their everyday life.

Perceptions, perceptions, perceptions. What's all this talk about perceptions? They are one of the "Ps" I use in psychotherapy. There are other "Ps" I use as well – I'll be getting to those. I want to emphasize right now that whatever I use in therapy with my clients they can take from therapy and use in their everyday lives – including the "Ps" of psychotherapy I'll be talking about. If my clients can do this so can you.

In the very first session I spend with my client, perceptions are inherently germane to what's happening. What's happening is a happening – between my client and myself – myself and my client. We are reciprocally perceiving one another. I am making perceptual judgments (another "P") about my client and my client is making them about me. My more perceptive clients probably are using all four aspects of person perception in perceiving me (without realizing it). I will not have gotten around to explaining that yet, but when I do they'll recognize, in retrospect, what they were perceptually using to "size me up"; and what I was relying upon to do the same with them. That's how we get at what the other's personality is like. Personality – (another "P") referring to that which distinguishes the person – their uniqueness – their one-of-a-kindness. No two personalities are exactly alike. We breathe a collective sigh of relief for this. Viva La difference!

A perception is a function of a presenter (another "P") and a perceiver ("P"). An interaction is a function of what each person (with their personality) brings to a given situation. The situation in this case is a client in psychotherapy with their therapist (me). My client is giving me their self-report about what is happening in their life. I'm listening to how they are saying what they're saying, to what they are saying. I'm also perceiving their appearance, body language, and facial expression. These are the four aspects of person perception one needs to pay attention to (to become an astute perceiver). Let me operationally define each of them for you:

- **Appearance** – What I see of a person that doesn't move

- **Mannerisms** – What I see of a person that does move

- **Voice Quality** – How one says what they say

- **Voice Content** – What one says

When all four are present, we may find ourselves relying on one more than the others in making our perceptual judgment. In some instances, one aspect may give us a perception that seemingly contradicts another. My research found that of the four aspects of person perception – Voice Quality i.e. How one says (tone, loud, soft, fast, slow, etc) was the most salient when making a perceptual judgment.

An example of **congruency** between two aspects would be an angry tone – speaking angry words. We also speak of congruency when we have one who is feeling angry speaking in an angry tone words of anger. But sometimes an **incongruency** occurs perceptually between one's feelings and one's mannerisms and tone. Such as in the case of someone with a passive aggressive personality who is red in the face banging their fist on the table shouting on the top of their voice, "I'm not angry." Incongruencies are especially interesting because inconsistencies in perceptual presentations have a way of grabbing our attention and encouraging us to dig deeper perceptually in trying to figure out what they're telling us about the person's personality.

If people were more congruent in their presentation it would make **perceptually judging** them a lot easier. Perhaps you don't like the way this sounds when I talk about perceptually judging someone. I want you to let the word perceptually ("P") influence your judgment about judging. The word judging otherwise may have negative connotations for you. Perceptual judgments should not be misconstrued as **value judgments**.

When two people are discussing what each has perceived taking place in a given situation (they found themselves in) each has their own perception of what happened, of what they saw and heard. Neither is better or worse, right or wrong. To say that the other's perception is wrong compared to yours would be to make a value judgment about a perceptual judgment. That would be the wrong thing to do. The upshot of this is that you and the other could discuss an event you shared ad infinitum (without even a smidgen of argument) so long as each of you respected the validity of the other's perceptual judgment (from their perspective) and, they – yours (from your perspective).

This is how I would like you to relate to each other whatever the subject matter you might be discussing together. One talks. The other listens. Then the other talks. And the other listens. Each has their own perspective. Each is wanting to feel that the other values their perspective. In so doing, you give the other the perspective that you value them (which can't help but raise the value they have to themselves).

See how this perception business works. Just by giving the other your undivided attention and listening to them intently and empathically the other perceives you as perceiving them as a person of worth – with something of value to say to them. Conversely, when one presents to the other like they're in pain because they have to listen and looks like they can hardly wait until it's over the presenter feels devalued by the other's perceived reaction. Even if one didn't consciously intend to give the other the perception they devalued the other's presentation (and taking it further – the other's person) – This is what realistically happened from the other's perspective.

If my client is the one who tells me the other interacts (using the word loosely) with them in the before-mentioned manner, my client is wanting to hear from me how I perceive such behavior. Keep in mind my client is sharing with me their perception of what took place. Their perception is reality as they experienced it. I accept their perception, therefore, as bona fide. If I were seeing this client as one of a couple I was treating (I don't treat couples unless both are willing to see me as individuals), I would, of course, upon seeing the other of the couple be able to get their perception of how it goes when the two of them interact. I'm quite sure I would be given two different perspectives of the same event (i.e. their interaction). [I would have gotten to the other's perception of their interaction (i.e. how it went between them) without sharing with them first what the other's perception had been – This for the obvious reason of not wanting to bias them].

If, however, I was pleasantly surprised to hear from the one a perspective that closely resembled the others. . . That the one had perceived themselves cut off and not listened to by the other – The other had independently pretty much told the same story and had a very similar perspective – Such confirmation provides an important starting point in helping them.

Can you see why I, as their couple and individual therapist, might get excited about this. – My perception of this is that we're making progress. The **one** is perceiving the **other** doing this. The **other** is perceiving themselves doing this – The **one** telling me this is what the **other** is doing. The **other** telling me, Yes this is what I'm doing. (Now we're getting somewhere.) The **one** who acknowledges, "Yes, I'm not a good listener, and I tend to interrupt, or cut the other off." But, -- (There's almost always a "but") the **other** should talk faster and get to their point quicker – It makes **them** nervous when the **other** takes so long.

An **admission** followed by a **defense** (Projection, Rationalization – Take your pick). Projection = The other's to blame for part of this.

Rationalization = These are plausible reasons I do what I do. An admission is no small thing. It may be the beginning of the **process of changing**. An admission suggests the individual is beginning to look at their behavior more objectively. This means they have begun to lower their defenses. They are starting to see themselves as they see others see them. It may also mean they are paying more attention to how their reaction to the other's presentation (their reaction being (itself) their presentation to the other), negatively affects the other's perception of their presentation (reaction).

Now that I've sufficiently confused you, let me try to clear things up this way. For every perception there's a presenter and a perceiver. The presenter presents. The perceiver reacts. Their reaction is in effect their presentation back to the other. Back and forth it goes until the interaction ceases. In the therapy room (especially when I put the couple together) perceptions are going on all over the place. Each is presenting to the other and to me. Directly to me. Indirectly to the other. It's like each is trying to talk to the other through me. I won't talk for them, but I will try to give them a safety net with my presence.

I prefer they look at the other when they are talking to them (i.e. have eye contact). When I see how hard it is for them to do this even though I'm there to support each of them as they try – I can only imagine what it must be like for them to talk to each other at home without my support. Maybe that's why in the beginning of couple therapy, one or the other, or both are telling me that this is something new they're experiencing in therapy – Looking at each other's face and eyes, whether talking or listening. I think it's important my couples learn to do this and practice this when they're home talking and listening to each other. Perceptually one misses so much of what's going on with the other when one looks down, past, or away from the other when talking or listening.

Eye contact when talking to someone or someone is talking to you in the therapy room goes like this. When clients first come to see me, they usually don't look at my face or eyes when they're talking to me. They look down or away. I attribute this to anxiety and a lack of self-confidence. Several sessions into their treatment, some of my clients look at my face and eyes when they talk to me. They're feeling more secure and self-confident – Like they're perceiving themselves at this point as having something of value to offer me. Most of my clients, however, right from the start look at me when I talk to them. ["Look at me when I'm talking to you" lurches somewhere in our hindbrain planted there by a father or a father figure. Maybe that's why they look at me when I talk to them.]

The important advice for you to take away from all of this is to look at the face and eyes of your other when you talk to them or listen to them. I'm not talking chit-chat here. I'm talking real talk, serious, meaningful, purposeful talk. What I'm not talking about when I'm talking about talking is saying something to the other who's in another room. Or trying to talk over the TV. Or when the kids are running around. Or when either one of you is too dead tired to give a damn. Find a time and place in your home – and do it. No excuses made. None accepted. Make it a regular thing once or twice a week. Subject matter? How about making it about the two of you (Boring! Did I hear someone say) – Make **that** then what the two of you talk about. Talk about perceptions, feelings, needs. Don't let initial awkwardness dissuade you. Do it on a regular basis and you'll desensitize yourselves to whatever anxiety you may be feeling. [Don't start your sentences with "You" … but with "I" … What this is getting at is when You use "You" you put the other on the defensive. With "I" you take ownership of what you're saying.]

I'm a staunch believer in the importance of each of you identifying what you need from the other and the relationship. I'd also like each of you to think about and put down on paper what you think the other needs. In fact each of you make two lists. – One with your needs on it – The other list with what you think the other's needs are. This is what I have the couples (I treat) do. One reads from their list of what they need. The other then reads from their list of what they thought the other needed. (Oh, I forgot to tell you, couples, out there – to rank order the needs on both your lists – (The highest priority needs at the top).

Intuitively you can see where I'm going with these lists. I'm trying to get each of you to think about what you need for yourself from the other and the relationship and see how this jives (or doesn't jive) with what the other thinks you need from them and the relationship. If these lists jive (relatively speaking) pretty well, you're in business – at least on paper.

In practice, however, it may be an entirely different story. By this I mean – Just because the other may have a pretty good idea of what you need from them doesn't mean you're getting it from them. Nor that you asserted to them what you needed. Nor if you did assert it, you got it. It might only mean that you two think along similar lines, even feel about things in a similar fashion – but that what's lacking is **behavioral change**, i.e. The doing thereof.

Mind-reading is the antithesis of assertiveness. Don't expect it from the other nor from yourself. Mind-reading is anathema to the person practicing person perception. One can't perceive what's in the other's mind. You may think you know what the other's thinking because you know them so well. But you don't know for sure. You can't know for sure. I'm talking about us regular people, not those who profess to be able to read minds. More power to them. But us, regular people, are better off not trying. It would probably only get us into trouble anyway.

Now, **Feeling** – perceptually – is a different matter. Using the aspects of person perception – Appearance and Mannerism, one is able to perceive feeling coming from the other even when they're not saying anything. People are generally pretty good at perceiving facial expressions in others: The happy face – The sad face – The angry face. These faces one could probably come to a general perceptual consensus about with other perceivers. There may be idiosyncratic differences connoting the before-mentioned **face feelings**. You or your other could be exceptions. In that case, maybe you've already come to know how, in particular, the other's face looks when feeling those feelings.

So it's agreed that one has a much better chance in reading feelings than mind thoughts. It also helps greatly when perceiving the other's feelings if the other is **congruent** – In the sense that what they're feeling inside pretty well matches up with what they're showing outside. Sometimes, people refer to this as "Wearing their feelings on their sleeve." If you're in a relationship with someone like this there's not much guesswork involved in figuring out what they're feeling. This is good from the standpoint of perceiving – making the other easier to read. Sometimes, however, feelings get out of control. The other emotes so much that all that feeling is hard for the other to handle. Also perceptually, the more the feelings come out doesn't necessarily mean the more they're feeling.

Some hold back their feelings, purposely. They may be afraid of their feelings. Or ashamed of their feelings. Or feel guilty about what they're feeling. Or they worry about what might happen to them, or the other, if they let their feelings out. So one's perception of what the other's feeling is seriously curtailed. I say seriously curtailed because perception of what they're feeling is not eliminated altogether. This is because one can think they're successfully hiding their feelings and yet the other is using the other aspects of person perception to (at least) get a feeling for what the other is feeling.

If I'm making perception sound like guesswork, it's really nothing of the sort. The more you practice person perception the better you'll get at it. When the other starts talking, you then have two more aspects of perception to draw from.

Remember the two – Voice Quality = How they say. Voice Content = What they say. Voice Quality, how they say what they say – their tone, loud, soft, harsh, mellow, angry, friendly will be a big help to you perceiving what the other's feeling. Voice Content, what they're saying should also help you figure out what they've been thinking and how they may be feeling.

Person perception is an art more than a science. Incidentally, this therapist views psychotherapy in the same light. I consider myself more an artist than a scientist. I've never had a problem with people from other disciplines calling psychology a "soft science." I particularly like the word "soft" as it pertains to what I do. A "hard" approach causes clients to hide behind the wall of their defenses or retreat deeper into the temporary safety of their shell. A "soft" approach invites clients to lower their defenses just a little and stick their neck out just a little from the shell they made for themselves.

What I'm trying to do with you, my reader, is to treat you as I would my clients, sharing with you what I would with my clients -- My knowledge and experience – particularly in the areas of personality and person perception. I've always been grateful these were my interests right from the start of my doctoral education and research and that I was able to bring what I learned and experienced to bear on the art I have practiced called psychotherapy.

I'm not suggesting you, my readers, try to become therapists to each other. For one thing, those who have tried this have found out the hard way it doesn't work. In fact it brings new problems into an already troubled relationship. But what I am hoping you will do is use what you learn about personality and perception from reading my books when you're perceiving the other. Trying to figure the other out. Thinking about what kind of response to make to the other. Wondering what you can do for the other. Mulling over what the other might need from you, etc. Almost everyone I know, and those I don't, practice "**armchair psychologizing**" – Meaning they fancy themselves as amateur psychologists. What I'm advocating for you is to be this in the best sense of the term in perceiving yourself and the other with whom you share your most important relationship.

Personality is that which distinguishes one person from another. You can use traits (adjectives) to describe a person's personality, or (my preference) – **needs** (which I find more dynamic than descriptive). If using a trait, one might perceive the other's personality as **authoritative**. If using a corresponding need one might perceive the other as having a **need to control**.

Needs can be large or small or yet undiscovered. If the need is too large or extreme it likely will dominate the person's personality. This will make life difficult for both the one having too large a need and the other who has a relationship with them. Often the one who has too large a need dominating their personality hooks up with another who has too large a need that is its polar opposite. E.g., One with an extreme need to care give. The other with an extreme need to be dependent and be taken care of. What could be better with regard to compatibility, you rhetorically ask. I suppose (even though I think it not healthy) it could "work" for both of them. But that would presume neither of them changed nor wanted anything to change. However, should either one move even a tiny bit away from the pole – trouble might start brewing. [I called the above arrangement – unhealthy – because in such a case of compatibility neither one would be inclined to grow – nor be encouraged to get in touch with what I call – The **other side of themselves** – And that's not healthy!]

Let me give you another example – Suppose you, through person perception, perceive the other as having a large need to nurture. And you perceive yourself as having a large need to be nurtured. Something's got to give if there are going to be changes regarding the status quo. Either the other begins to assert their need to be nurtured or you (on your own) having perceived yourself as you typically are in this regard begin to nurture (If not on your own, then in response to what the other asserted).

No matter how perceptive you think you are – i.e., You're really gaining confidence that you can perceive what the other needs – It still would be a far better thing for the other, the relationship, and even you, if the other identified for themselves what they needed and then asserted it to you for your serious consideration. The margin of misperceiving what the other needs is reduced to zero when the other owns what they need and puts it out there, openly, honestly, and directly. The ball then is clearly in your court and whatever your response – It's yours to own. If your response is Yes, I can give you that. Or even if you qualify your response with an I can try to fulfill that need – You have essentially committed yourself to observable behavioral change.

If your response is I can't give you that but I'm willing to give you this – Then this is what you have asserted to the other. It then behooves the other to assert back to you whether what you have offered is acceptable. And so it may go, back and forth, until a compromise is reached that both of you can commit yourselves to in **words** and **action**.

When one asserts, it empowers the one who does it. The process of identifying one's need and feeling worthy enough to own it. Seeing it as very important to your person. Putting it out there perceptually with a serious face and a strong voice – is self-edifying. You've done your part, if you will. It likely took courage and determination in some instances. But you did it. Of that you may be rightfully proud.

I can't recall any of the thousands of clients I've seen who couldn't use some **assertiveness training**. Think about what you want to say. How you want to say it. Don't start out by saying "You"...which will probably put the other immediately on the defensive (which, believe me, you don't want to do). Put it out there in the first person by starting your sentence with "I." You're taking ownership of what you're about to say. That's the way it should be. No assigning blame to the other. Certainly no attacking the other for not knowing or giving you what you needed.

But this is only Phase-One of a Two-Phase Process of Asserting. The second phase is the one my clients found problematic. I'm referring to the nature of the response they got – especially if the other was unaccustomed to the one asserting. Bottom line, the response was not the kind they were looking for. Responses ranged from no response (which is still a response), to "Maybe, I'll have to think about it and get back to you," to a flat-out "No."

When they brought me their report about how they asserted and what they got as a response for their effort (and, believe me they weren't a "happy camper") they were respectfully put out with me for having encouraged them to assert in the first place. While I empathized with them regarding what had happened to them and gave them time to lick their wounds, my mercy ended there. I took the Frank Sinatra approach with them – Pick yourself up. Dust yourself off. And do it over again.

Reassert, reassert, reassert. Don't rationalize away something that originally was important to you. Remember, don't expect the other to know what you need – even if the other is unusually perceptive, and you're consciously trying to give them perceptual cues (other than talking, that is). But, either they're not picking them up. Or, they're not interested. Or they're consciously trying to get you to speak. For the individual's, and the couple's sake, I want them to assert. If for no other reason than that neither of them will be able to say later on – I had no idea the other felt that way – Or needed that from me – They never said anything about it. [They won't be able to shift responsibility that way].

Think of a scenario where you and the other are in a relationship in which both of you have made the commitment to each other to practice the art of assertiveness whenever, wherever possible – Speaking to each other using "I" – Putting your thoughts, feelings, needs out there directly, openly, honestly for the other's consideration. Assert, reassert,

assert back and forth. Negotiate. Compromise. Commit to. And act accordingly.

But unless you have that kind of relationship where mutual assertiveness is going on, on an ongoing basis, you and the other would do well to practice the **Art** of **Person Perception**. A perceptive person can get a lot of information about the other without the other saying anything. Facial expression, mannerisms, posture, observable behaviors offer up **Perceptual Cues** that you can use to figure out what the other may be feeling or needing.

Especially can you trust your perceptions if the other has shown a behavioral pattern when they are feeling a particular feeling. In other words, the other has the habit of giving off the same perceptual cues associated with that feeling. You perceived the cues and found out later on what the feeling was that came with them. E.g. the slouching in the chair. The eyes staring into space – downward case. The heavy sighs. The saying not a word, meant – Very tired or depressed.

How you then respond to the perceptual cues the other gives off is the key to whether or not an interaction takes place between you and the other. And if there is an interaction what kind it will be. A lot will depend on how the other perceives you. How the other perceives you will depend on how you present yourself to the other – And how you present yourself may well depend on how you are feeling about the other you're perceiving – And how the other feels about you presenting.

Sounds complicated doesn't it, all these perceptions going on to worry about. When I break it down for you hopefully it will make sense to you. Let's say in the before-mentioned example the other is feeling worn out. Bushed. It's been one of those days. The other felt harried and rushed. Too much to do. Too many interruptions. (You know how it goes) – So there – The other is in the chair – looking as I have described. What to do if you're the one perceiving the other. If you've perceived the other like this before, your experience in this situation should help you decide what to do next, or what not to do next; (one would think so at least.) Would that the other's response be that predictable! However, you've learned from experience that even though the perceptual cues are there giving you a pretty good idea of what the other's feeling, there's still the question of what they're in touch with needing. And even if they know what they need whether they'll accept anything from you.

So once again it sounds complicated. What to do? Choices: Hon, you really looked bushed – like you've had a rough day (This could have been at work or home or both.) Do you want to talk about it, I'll be glad to just listen. Hon, you really look like you need a hug and I'm the one to give it to you. How about a back rub, or a neck rub. Why don't you just sit there and relax and I'll take care of whatever you planned on doing.

If none of these work? – (Of course you're not going to offer them all on the same occasion). You probably would be getting some response before you went down your list anyway. Besides, going through all of them until you hit one would be too much for the other (in their state) to think about. So you put one or two out there and see if there's a taker. The other might go for one. If so, you follow through and see what happens.

You, of course, could right at the start simply ask the other what they need – Or better, what you can do for them. Sometimes the response that comes back is "Nothing," – Especially if the other is typically non-assertive – Or, if the other has the type of personality that has trouble asking for anything or receiving anything.

Some of us, unfortunately, may be so preoccupied with our own problems and concerns – Or ourselves be like the other – bushed and worn down – that we miss the perceptual cues the other is giving off. So, the one occasion we do pay attention and get "out of ourselves" our offer comes as an unexpected surprise and catches the other off-guard.

Then there's the case of the other who perhaps has (unbeknownst to us) been feeling neglected and they're upset about this. So they're not going to make it easy for us to be for them. Therefore, their response contradicts their perceptual cues – "Punishing" us for our past neglect and playing the martyr card by saying – There's nothing we can do for them. (Does any of this sound familiar)?

Again, my premise is – Assert to the other that you are ready and willing to help the other – in whatever way or manner they decide. At least put it out there. If they turn you down there's little if anything you can do about it. The need they may be asserting is – to be left alone. Since you can't read their mind you oblige them with the parting word – If you change your mind, please let me know.

Here's an opportunity for you to be **Proactive** (another "P") if you care to be. What this means is that you take the initiative following your perceptual cues and get into a behavior you think will possibly satisfy at least one of the other's needs. Unless, of course the other is adamant about being left alone. Then you give them what they want (even though it may not be in reality what they want). You don't really want to force the issue. Nor do you want to reinforce the other's behavior of saying one thing but feeling another. The other needs to learn to assert. Don't buy into the other's comment when they say things like – You should know what I want. I shouldn't have to tell you. This represents the other taking the easy way out – And putting their responsibility on you.

That's one of one's favorite defenses – To say they don't care when they do – It's called **Reaction Formation**. The person using this defense does not subscribe to the statement – Say what you mean and mean what you say. The person who says "No" when they mean "Yes" – How do you deal with this kind of behavior! – Not well. I suppose if it happens often enough that it becomes a behavioral pattern, one's odds would be stacked in favor of taking the "No" for a "Yes." But the one time you proceed on that basis you could be mistaken. So the best thing to do (if you can) is to validate with the other what they **really** are saying and meaning.

Validating is part of the assertiveness process as well as part of the art of person perception. It works like this – Suppose you're perceiving your other and all the perceptual cues available to you are lining up to give you one perceptual conclusion – That the other is angry! I've chosen anger as an example of what one is perceiving because anger with all the prominent perceptual cues it gives off is probably one of the easiest feelings to perceive. However, in this case – Validating would not first concern itself with whether the other is angry (or not). But one would be validating with the other – At what, or about what, or with whom, the other is angry.

Too often one makes perceptual assumptions – Like the other is angry at me – When in reality that's not the case at all. It's important one doesn't jump to conclusions in cases like this. Typically one doesn't handle the other's anger that well. Even worse if one thinks it's directed at them. If based on one's perception that the other is angry, one reacts like they're already in trouble. And, defensively goes on the offensive. The other's anger, which initially may have had nothing to do with you may become directed at you in a hurry. [The caveat is directed at one's perceptual inclination to assume that when the other is angry, they must be angry **at them** for something they said, or did, or didn't do. – However, if they were to validate with the other the reality of what's going on with the other and say something to this effect – I can see you're angry about something – If you want to talk about it I'm here to listen – Their assumption made may prove unfounded.]

You basically can use the same approach with the other who's angry – Whether it turns out they're angry or not – I can see you're angry – I don't know whether you're angry with me or something else – In either case, I'm here to listen, if you want to talk about it. Validating in this manner helps you, the perceiver, not immediately go on the defensive – and what would be worse – go on the offensive. And helps the other, the presenter, take the edge off their anger and calm down a bit by having someone to talk to who is willing to listen.

Remember it's the other's anger one is talking about here. They have the right to feel what they feel – to express it if they so choose. You have the prerogative to choose to listen or not to listen – Especially if the anger is, for certain, directed at you. Validating in this case would mean you would say something like this – I can see you're angry at me. But right now when you're as angry as you seem to be, I would be willing to listen to what you have to say – if you could tone it down a little bit. If you need time to collect yourself a bit, why don't you do that. And then you can talk and I will listen. [What this is getting at is unless you're a masochist it's not your obligation to stand under the fan while you-know-what is hitting it]

I cannot stress enough how important validating is to the process of person perception. When validation precedes reaction, (which of course, is what the perceiver strives for) what can result is a reaction tempered by the realization that feelings are not the same as acting on those feelings. That at a feeling level, before they commence into actions there is still time to talk and listen. And actions stopped before they start.

- You sound like you're running out of patience; I don't blame you; How about I try it for a while.

- Why don't you rest for a while and maybe you'll feel better.

- Why not let me take over. You've done enough for one day.

- You look like you could stand some help. Let me pitch in.

- What's going on? Did something happen at work, you really look anxious.

Validating your perceptions of the other with the other. Giving the other an opportunity to share with you – whatever they're feeling about whatever happened – or didn't happen. Offering to spell them. Or just to get their feelings out.

Problems arise, however, based on how the other perceives themselves, perceives how you are perceiving them, and perceiving you. If the other, as too often is the case, perceives themselves as having not been up to the task at hand (and are thinking they should have been). And then they perceive in your comments and offers an insinuation that you are perceiving them as they are already perceiving themselves. And perceive you as sounding like you are perceiving yourself, in this instance, superior to them. The sum total of their perceptions will probably mean – They will turn down the help you're offering them. And press on. Or get off track. And start to debate with you what your thoughts were about them when you made the offer in the first place. See how complicated things can become based on the different perceptions they have of a given situation. Validating as the two of you go along in your interaction will help straighten out misunderstandings to some extent – But often not enough to satisfy both your perceptions.

Sometimes I think it works just as well, if not better, to just go ahead, get proactive and do some of the things that still need doing – That the other, for whatever reason, didn't get to. Even if this means they're perceiving a message you didn't send in the first place (at least from your perspective). When you do things (that are perceptually observable by the other) the other (who used to do these things maybe pretty much by themselves) eventually, hopefully, will realize none of this was done to one-up them or show them up. Or suggest they were not capable of doing it on their own. But rather as part of a new realization.

That in a relationship responsibilities are shared. In effect very few responsibilities in a relationship have only **One Name** on them.

Let's talk personality for a while and then tie it in with person perception and behavioral change. I like to ask my couples when I see them individually (which I always do i.e. see my couples also as individuals or I won't see them as a couple) – what they perceive the other's personality to be like. They're free to describe the other using traits (adjectives) or needs (need to be, need to do). Relatively speaking they do better with traits than needs. But, in reality, they don't do "so hot" with either.

How would you fare if I were to ask you to describe your other's personality? What's your other like? – Trait-wise: Hard/Soft. Loud/Quiet. Strong/Weak. Friendly/Unfriendly. Patient/Impatient. Sensitive/Insensitive. (You can keep the list going on your own with what you've perceived of the other). The traits are presented as essentially polar opposites. But I want you to know there's a lot of "gray area" in between each pairing – (Where your perception of your other's personality may more realistically belong).

If you were to use needs to describe your other's personality, what would you come up with? Need to care take. Need to be right. Need to do well. Need to control. (You can add to this list too as it pertains to your perception of your other). If you were one of my clients you'd get help from me with this. I'd have my own perceptions of the personality traits or needs (My preference is Needs) of each of you to share with each of you – yours and the others.

So what's the benefit – the **efficacy** – of perceiving the personality needs of the other? Suppose your other has a large need to control their physical and human environment. You perceive this need as you observe the other reacting to something, or someone that/who is not cooperating – Frustration Personified!

Sometimes you're on the receiving end of their need to control and you don't like it one bit. You perceive it. You can't miss it. It's in the other's face. Their gestures. Their tone. Their words. You can feel the control emanating from the other, filling the atmosphere with tension. The key, here, is – You have to perceive it before you can do anything about it.

Okay. So you perceive your other as a controlling person. So what! What can you do about it anyway? Well, of course, if you're a person who has a large need to be controlled i.e. you depend on the other to call the shots and when they do you get angry at them for doing it – Then you're content to leave things as they are.

However, if you're a person who doesn't like to be controlled (and that's putting it mildly) then you'll want to know what, if anything, you can do to turn things around (at least forty-five degrees or so). You can start by letting the other know how you are feeling when you perceive them controlling you. Remember, it's what you perceive as reality that is contributing to the way you're feeling. Don't let the other talk you out of what you're perceiving and feeling. The perception and the feeling are yours.

I'm not trying to control you, the other may say in response. And certainly it's possible the controlling side of the other has become such a dominant part of their personality that it has become their MO for interacting. It's an automatic habitual behavioral pattern that they really don't give much thought to and very little, if any, consideration regarding the other's feeling.

The efficacy of you owning the feeling the controlling one has precipitated in you and putting it in "I-form" and asserting how you feel is that it can very well precipitate a dialogue between you and the other that might otherwise not have occurred. If a dialogue commences and then or at a later time, each of you is able to own your part in how the interaction went down – That will be a very important first step in changing presentations and perceptions.

The controlling one would have to be open to perceiving themselves as the other perceives them. And lowering their defenses perceive themselves as objectively as they can to identify what aspects of person perception are giving the other the perception of "controlling." It could be facial expression, body language, tone or content (or any combination of the four). The one who has perceived the other as controlling can pitch in and indicate to the other what they perceived in the other's presentation as controlling. If there is concurrence between their respective perceptions then the controlling one will know what to work on.

But you ask, what is there for the one who felt controlled to change? There's plenty. For starters, there may be characteristics in their personality, which in their presentation trigger controlling tendencies in the other – Over-dependency for one. Literally crying out "Control me." Passivity for another, which presents as "Take over, I'm not up for doing it."

Do you see how this works in an interaction such as we've been talking about? An interaction is a function of what each brings to a given situation. In our case in point, one who presents "Take Over" meeting up with the other with controlling tendencies. Talk about reciprocal reinforcement. This is a classic! Simplistic, in theory anyway, (more complicated in practice) – The one needs to become less dependent, less passive. The other less controlling. These modifications showing up in their respective presentation and perception.

You can take this paradigm for changing presentations and perceptions and apply it to other interactions between you and the other in which your different personalities come together. For example, one of you may be satisfied with a task half-done, left for another day. In so being and so doing, you present to the other – Who tenaciously sticks with a task no matter what or how long it takes – until it's done. And guess how your presentation is perceived by the other? You don't have to guess. You'll probably find out in a hurry so nothing's left to guesswork. The perceptions of your presentation range from: – Here we go again – a job half-done. I wonder how long I'll have to live with this mess this time. I'd fall over if the other ever finished what they started one time. The other knows how I feel about doing things "half-ass" but they do it anyway. I'm sick of being put in this position where either I have to finish what they started, or live with it like it is, for God only knows how long.

Follow the paradigm and you can take it from here. If it goes like in the first example in which control was the issue – Then in this case, the issue is how each approaches and proceeds with a project that needs to be done – The way one hopes it will go. There'll be dialogue. In this case, much earlier in the process, when the project is first discussed, as to who is going to do what. How it's going to be done. When it's going to be done. At that point each gives their input and each gives their honest reply to the other's input. Differences in the what, how, and when are duly noted and a compromise hopefully reached that both can commit to. As to how it will all play out from the beginning to the end – I think it's safe to assume the perceptions of each other's presentations throughout the project will not be in perfect accord.

In our example, the one used to stopping at some point and leaving the rest for another day may work at it longer to get more of it done the first time – and then commit to finishing it up the very next weekend. The other tries to perceive the process differently than before, trying their best to modify their need to see it completed the first time, and keeps any thoughts or feelings contrariwise to themselves. A perfect solution for either or both – No way! But then, perfect solutions are not a part of our reality – at least they won't be if we're in touch with reality.

So much for this subject. Let's put it to rest and for the remainder of my book I want to talk to you about how to manage person perceptions – Specifically perceptions of yourself and perceptions you perceive the other to have of you.

Managing person perceptions. What am I talking about? By now you should understand what person perception is all about. So what remains to explain is what I mean by **managing**, and then specifically, **managing person perceptions**. **Managing** – I might as well tell it like it is, I'm talking about **working** person perceptions in such a way that one is able to increase the probability that they will be perceived by others the way they want to be and perceive themselves the way they want to be = **Manipulation in its Highest Psychotherapeutic Sense**.

I begin with the premise that one's self-concept i.e. the picture they see when they look at themselves was painted by one's perceptions of how others perceived them. [Without changes that would continue to be the case.] How one feels about the picture they see is their self-worth.

When you look at yourself, **really** look at yourself, what do you see? Do you like what you see overall? Are there some things you see you don't like? Are there some characteristics you would like to have more of, less of; some you'd like to see that you don't see yet? [Lots to look for. Lots to think about. Take your time. Don't be in a hurry. The most important thing about perceiving yourself is that you be as **honest** and as **real** as you can be].

Let's suppose when you look at yourself you see the characteristic – **Caring**. Assuming you like this about yourself – Then the only question to ask yourself is whether you would like to be **more** caring than you already are. Before you would give this an automatic – Of course (because everyone could stand to be more caring) – You may be one who because of what you've already experienced in your life actually think it would be better for you to be a little less caring. For one thing maybe then others would not find you as easy to take advantage of. So even though you like this about yourself you'd like a little less of it.

On the I-don't-like-what-I-see-side, you may see in your picture the characteristic of **Intolerance**. This manifests itself to you when you see how quickly and intensely you react when the other deviates from the standard you've set for them. You pounce on the other's **relatively minor** departure from your norm as you would in **punishing betrayal**. After the fact, when you reflect upon your behavior you can hardly stand yourself for perpetrating on the other such a gross overreaction.

Suppose for whatever reason you would like to see yourself as **assertive**. However, when you look at the picture of yourself – the painter left that out. What does this mean? It means you can not see it because it has yet to be discovered. It wasn't reflected back to you earlier in your life as being perceived in you by others – for whatever reason. You have yet to see it in the way you see others see you.

So in our examples we have one who when they perceive themselves as **caring** would like to be less caring – Perceive themselves as **intolerant** and would like to be less intolerant (or more tolerant) and perceiving none of it as yet, would like the characteristic of **assertiveness**.

Might one just as well ask for the moon, as believe that one can change the picture of themselves in just the way they want to. But I'm here to tell you it can be done. How? You ask? By managing perceptions. Managing perceptions involves **Manipulation in its Highest Psychotherapeutic Sense**.

The process starts with you validating with your other whether their perception of you regarding the three characteristics we came up with in our example jives with your perception of yourself. If it does, then you're on your way. If it doesn't then revisit your perception of yourself once more just to double check. If the picture is the same as before, go with your perception rather than the other's perception of you and work on making the changes you think you'd like to make.

Managing perceptions means manipulating perceptions until one achieves perceptions of themselves they want to see when they look at themselves; and their perception of themselves jives with how they perceive others are perceiving them. Managing perceptions involves eventually making behavioral changes. Behavioral changes come about when one gains insights about what behavioral changes they need to make in order to change their presentation to achieve the perception they want to give of themselves to others and themselves.

When one is in psychotherapy the whole process of managing perceptions is made easier because I can give the insights to the client about what of their present behaviors needs changing – and also what kind of new behaviors they would need to get into to achieve in their presentation the new perception they want to give.

The toughest one of the three characteristics in our example to want to change would be to change caring into being perceived as less caring. Caring is such a positive characteristic for others and ourselves to perceive and is reinforced by the positive responses that perceivers make to presenters of it. The motivation to change to less caring has already been alluded to; i.e. when one presents as one who cares too much; others with cares and concerns are attracted to the one who cares; and it usually turns into a one-way street with no chance for the one who cares to get any of their needs met (other than their need to care, that is). To present as less caring one may have to say, No, once in a while to someone to whom up to now they've always said, Yes. I'm sorry, but I can't help you, may have to be added to their repertoire of responses. How about I talk about what's been bothering me for a change and you do the listening!

There will be fallouts from making such perceptual changes. Those who were drawn to you before, you won't hear from. Those who only wanted to take from you and give nothing in return may not come around anymore. In dealing with their differential responses to your new behavioral changes (perceptually manifested in your new presentations) think of it this way – The fallout (in this case fall-away) is more on them than you. They are not able to absorb the change and bottom-line find no more reason to relate to you if they cannot use you in this way. Those who were not relating to you only to use you in this way – having changed their perception of you hopefully will hang in there with you – and your relationship with them will become more reciprocal and less one-sided.

In sharp contrast you'll find that when you're able to modify the characteristic of intolerance (and in that process become more tolerant, and less judgmental) – You'll change your presentation. When you're in situations where priorly you punished others who did not measure up to your standards of performance (with after-the-fact, caustic criticisms) – now you'll extend encouragement and praise for the effort expended and offer constructive criticism only if it's asked for – and even then be gentle.

I think by now you can see that in order to know what behavioral changes to make – and how to make them – you need first to reflect upon the changes you will need to make in your presentation to achieve this end. Let me suggest to you how to go about gathering information you can use in changing your presentation – One thing you can do is honestly and objectively reflect on your behavior of the past when you interacted with your other (for example, shall we say when you presented your intolerant side). I dare say if you replay your part in your mind, doing and saying pretty much the opposite of what you did and said, this will do quite nicely in facilitating a much improved presentation and perception.

Or, you can closely observe someone else that you would perceive behaves in a tolerant and nonjudgmental way when they interact with you and others and take perceptual cues from them that you can use in your new presentation. Remember, this is an art form you are learning, so models for the behavioral changes you want to make are appropriate. Without announcing any of this ahead of time, practice presenting yourself as a more tolerant person with your other (at the first opportunity). Slowly desensitize yourself to the newness of the process and any anxiety coming with it.

Keep in mind this is new for your other too. The other is more accustomed to the old you, so their set of responses may not at all fit very well your expectations. Don't let this dissuade you. Keep presenting in the new way and eventually you'll be perceiving in your perceptions of the other's perception of you what you have been working on presenting.

We talked about coming up with a characteristic that wasn't part of the picture we had of ourself before. Assertiveness is the characteristic one was looking for. Again if you're not in therapy, you can read about what it entails in books like mine. Once you have an idea about what assertive behavior looks like, then look for it displayed by others.

You'll find that assertiveness has to do with being in control of oneself. Taking responsibility and ownership of one's thoughts and feelings. Using the first person "I." Putting your needs out there for the other's consideration directly – openly, honestly. Dealing with whatever response you get from the other. Remember, if you haven't asserted before it will be new to you and your other. Prepare yourself to persevere. The first part of assertiveness is to put it out there. The second part is hanging in there and negotiating and compromising with the other so that you at least get something of what you were asking for.

So what do I say to my critics who take exception to my contention that managing perceptions is an art form. It is efficacious in that by changing one's presentation one can change the other's perception – can change the way they perceive the other perceives them – can change the way they perceive themselves. I figure out the way to present myself to the other so that the probability of their perceiving me the way I want them to perceive me is high (keeping in mind the variance of perception their personality brings to the situation). Thus I am managing perceptions by the behavioral changes I present. Critics would say this is nothing more than unabashed manipulation. They would question the authenticity of a well thought-out and practiced presentation. To which I reply…Balderdash!

Think about it for a minute. Isn't this the way we learned how to present ourselves very early in our lives. We presented. Our parents or parent substitutes perceived. We perceived their perception of our presentation. If we perceived they were pleased, we repeated said presentation without change. If we perceived they were not pleased, with their help and guidance and using them as models, we changed our presentation in order to perceive ourselves the way we thought they wanted to perceive us.

Is any of this managing of perceptions unauthentic? I think not! Managing perceptions is the way we make behavioral changes. And we use these behavioral changes in our presentations to manage perceptions. I could use terms like stimulus –

response – stimulus connections and reinforcements – and make it sound more "scientific" – but I won't. To me psychotherapy is an art form – As is person perception.

We are, all of us, artists in our own right painting the picture of ourselves from our perception of other's perceptions of us. As we look at our picture of ourselves we see parts of it we would like to enhance, parts we would like to diminish, and there may be a new part we would like to add that we don't see yet. This is all part of our growing process which continues throughout our life.

In Sum

Some say psychotherapy is for the weak. These same individuals probably also would say that to need is to be weak. I say it is a weakness not to need. Therapy is to help people help themselves. Who in this life couldn't stand a little help. To make the weak less weak. To make the strong, stronger.

People often turn to therapy when there's a crisis in their life. This is good. I'm glad they come. I'm glad they're not too proud. I'm glad they're not too ashamed. I'm honored that they trust me with their problem.

Some of these, when the crisis is over, they're gone. There's no more need from their perspective. I see the need, but they don't. I wish them well, and off they go, until the next crisis.

I wish more people would come to therapy just to grow – psychologically healthy people wanting to become even healthier.

Whether you are in therapy, have been in therapy, or are presently contemplating therapy, my message to you is the same. . . Personality's characteristics are pretty much in place by age six. They develop by person perception and self-experience. Personality characteristics can be modified – What we have too much of we can have less of. What we have too little of we can have more of. We can discover characteristics we haven't seen yet. We can gain insights by lowering our defenses and trusting our perceptions. We can make behavioral changes by changing our presentation which will result in our changing the perceptions others have of us – the perceptions we have of how others perceive us – perceptions of ourselves. To expand our personality and grow our lives it is important that we learn and practice the **art** of (to realize the **efficacy** of) **managing person perceptions**.

Blessings
Take Good Care,
Doc Ken
K. L. Fischer, PhD

THE ART AND EFFICACY OF MANAGING
PERSON PERCEPTIONS

About the Author

- Dr. Kenneth L. Fischer (affectionately called Doc Ken) has been in helping professions his entire adult life.

- Founder and pastor of Peace Lutheran Church, Disco, MI

- Pastor of Mt. Olive Lutheran Church, Grand Rapids, MI

- Junior High School teacher 8th grade English, 9th grade Latin, Muskego, MI

- First psychologist in the history of the Men's Unit, State Prison, Lowell, FL

- Dr. Fischer received his PhD in Personality Psychology, Michigan State University, East Lansing, MI

- His doctoral work was in Person Perception

- An instructor and lecturer, Dept. of Psychology, University of Wisconsin, Milwaukee, WI

- Also taught at various colleges throughout the Milwaukee-Metro area, namely Milwaukee Area Technical College, Mt. Mary College, Alverno College, and at Carthage College, Racine, WI

- Dr. Fischer has been a practicing psychologist in his own clinic for the past thirty-five years, treating adult couples and individuals

☐ His areas of expertise are in Personality and Person Perception

☐ His specialty is Personality Disorders

☐ Support Therapy Clinic is located in Hartland, WI

Other Books by Kenneth L. Fischer, PhD

Closeness Without Control:
The Key To A Loving Reciprocal Relationship Of
Assertive Independent Equals

Seeing Ourselves As We See Others See Us:
Our Personality Develops Through Person Perception
and Self-Experience

The Gray Area Of Psychological Abuse:
Abusee? Abuser? Or Both? How Can We Tell?
What Can We Do?

**Psychologically Speaking What Are We
Really Saying?**
The Music Behind The Music Behind Our Words

Don't Like The Way It Is - Change It:
Changing Before Or After An Ultimatum

We've Got Personality!
Now What?

Don't Be A Stranger (To Yourself):
Go Outside Yourself To Get Inside Yourself Then Turn
Yourself Inside Out

In Defense Of Defensiveness:
Knowing Our Defenses, Lowering Our Defenses,
Living With Our Defenses

The Incomparable Spunkerface and Company:
Heaven Sent - Heaven Bent

Lamenting The Loss of Loyalty:
Where Has All The Loyalty Gone?!